Rookie National Parks™

Grand Canyon National Park

by Lisa M. Herrington

Content Consultant

Nanci R. Vargus, Ed.D.
Professor Emeritus, University of Indianapolis

Reading Consultant

Jeanne M. Clidas, Ph.D.
Reading Specialist

Children's Press®
An Imprint of Scholastic Inc.

Library of Congress Cataloging-in-Publication Data
Names: Herrington, Lisa M., author.
Title: Grand Canyon National Park/by Lisa M. Herrington.
Description: New York, NY: Children's Press, an imprint of Scholastic Inc., 2018. |
Series: Rookie national parks | Includes bibliographical references and index.
Identifiers: LCCN 2016051660| ISBN 9780531233320 (library binding: alkaline
paper) | ISBN 9780531239049 (paperback: alkaline paper)
Subjects: LCSH: Grand Canyon National Park (Ariz.)—Juvenile literature.
Classification: LCC F788 .H48 2018 | DDC 979.1/32—dc23
LC record available at https://lccn.loc.gov/2016051660

Produced by Spooky Cheetah Press
Design: Judith Christ-Lafond/Brenda Jackson/Joan Michael

Published in 2018 by Children's Press, an imprint of Scholastic Inc.

Printed in China 62

SCHOLASTIC, CHILDREN'S PRESS, ROOKIE NATIONAL PARKS™, and
associated logos are trademarks and/or registered trademarks of Scholastic Inc.,
557 Broadway, New York, NY 10012.

1 2 3 4 5 6 7 8 9 10 R 27 26 25 24 23 22 21 20 19 18

Photographs ©: cover: tonda/iStockphoto; back cover: EURASIA PRESS/Media
Bakery; 1-2: PCRex/Shutterstock; 3: Mark Sykes/Getty Images; 4-5: Danita
Delimont Stock/AWL Images; 6 center: Stefano Politi Markovina/AWL Images;
6-7: Ian Dagnall/Alamy Images; 8: Prochasson Frederic/Dreamstime; 10-11:
Momatiuk-Eastcott/Getty Images; 12 top: Eric Hanson/Getty Images; 12-13:
Mark Peter Drolet/Getty Images; 14: Kerrick James/Getty Images; 15: Michael
DeYoung/age fotostock; 16: Jeff Foott/Getty Images; 17: Ralph Lee Hopkins/
Getty Images; 18 top: Kevin Schafer/Minden Pictures; 18 bottom: CSP_peterwey/
age fotostock; 19: mandj98/iStockphoto; 20-21: Wild Horizon/Getty Images;
21: David DesRochers Photography/Animals Animals; 22-23: John Warburton-
Lee/AWL Images; 24-25: John Burcham/Getty Images; 25: Jack Kurtz/ZUMA
Press/Newscom; 26 squirrel: Art Directors & TRIP/Alamy Images; 26 raven:
Jakgree/iStockphoto; 26 bobcat: KEVIN SCHAFER/age fotostock; 26 porcupine:
Isselee/Dreamstime; 26 coyote: Outdoorsman/Dreamstime; 26 condor: Steve
Johnson/Getty Images; 26 deer: Rinus Baak/Dreamstime; 27 elk: Josef Pittner/
Shutterstock; 27 rabbit: D. Robert & Lorri Franz/Getty Images; 27 sheep:
KenCanning/iStockphoto; 27 lizard: Joel Sartore/Getty Images; 27 trout:
tab1962/iStockphoto; 27 bat: Michael Durham/Minden Pictures; 27 eagle:
withgod/iStockphoto; 27 ringtail: Mitsuyoshi Tatematsu/Minden Pictures; 27
rattlesnake: Amwu/Dreamstime; 30 top left: vkbhat/iStockphoto; 30 top right:
Mike Cavaroc/Alamy Images; 30 bottom left: Robert J Erwin/Getty Images; 30
bottom right: Dorling Kindersley/Getty Images; 31 canyon: Prochasson Frederic/
Dreamstime; 31 crevices: mandj98/iStockphoto; 31 park: kavram/Shutterstock;
31 rim: Mark Peter Drolet/Getty Images; 32: july7th/iStockphoto.

Maps by Jim McMahon.

Table of Contents

Introduction

I am Ranger Red Fox, your tour guide. Are you ready for an amazing adventure in the Grand Canyon?

Welcome to Grand Canyon National Park!

The Grand Canyon was made a **national park** in 1919. People visit national parks to explore nature.

The Grand Canyon is in Arizona. The park covers more than one million acres! That is about the size of Delaware.

United States

Arizona

Grand Canyon
National Park

N
W—E
S

Desert View
Watchtower

What a view!
You can see for miles from
the tower's overlook.

The Grand Canyon has incredible scenery. It has steep hiking trails, colorful rocks, and a winding river. It also has amazing plants and animals.

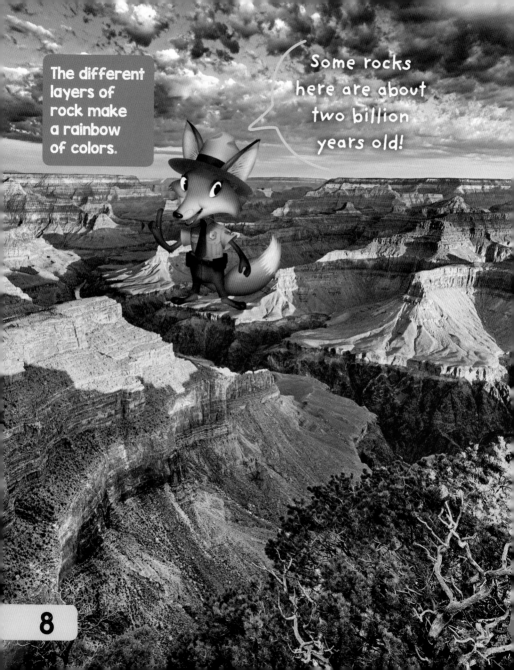

The different layers of rock make a rainbow of colors.

Some rocks here are about two billion years old!

Chapter 1

A Canyon That Rocks

The Grand Canyon looks like a big hole in the earth. But a **canyon** is really a deep, narrow valley with steep sides. Its walls are made from layers of rock.

The Colorado River runs along the bottom of the Grand Canyon. Over millions of years, its water has worn away the rock. It carved out the canyon.

There is a reason this canyon is called "grand"!

Sandstone cliffs tower above the Colorado River.

10

The Grand Canyon is one of the biggest canyons in the world. It is 277 miles (446 kilometers) long. At its widest point, the canyon is 18 miles (29 km) across. In some spots, it is nearly a mile (1.6 km) to the bottom. That is like standing on top of almost four Empire State Buildings!

It is a challenging hike to the snowy North Rim.

More than five million people visit the park every year.

Visitors flock to Mather Point on the South Rim.

Chapter 2

From Top to Bottom

The **rim** makes up the top edges of the canyon. The park is divided into the North Rim and the South Rim. The North Rim is higher and colder than the South Rim. It gets more rain and snow. Travel is harder there.

Most people explore the park from the South Rim. There are many lookout points. These are good places to take photos.

Mules have been carrying Grand Canyon visitors since the 1880s.

It is not an easy trip to the bottom of the canyon. You need to take steep, winding trails to get there. Some people hike the trails. Others ride down on mules. The temperature gets warmer as you go farther down. Near the bottom it is like a desert.

Visitors set up tents to sleep at the bottom of the canyon.

It is hard to go to the bottom and back up in one day. Most people spend the night.

Chapter 3

That's Wild!

The plants and landscape change from the canyon's top to bottom, too. Ponderosa pines, Douglas firs, and spruce trees grow on the rim. Cactus plants and desert wildflowers are found on the dry canyon floor.

Many evergreens grow along the North Rim.

More than 1,700 types of plants grow in and around the canyon.

Prickly pear cactus blooms brighten the bottom of the canyon in spring.

The park is also home to a wide range of animals. Elk, coyotes, and bobcats roam the land. Bighorn sheep graze on the cliffs. Lizards crawl into **crevices** below. Rainbow trout and other fish swim in the river.

Bobcats usually hunt at night.

Visitors are likely to see mule deer in the park.

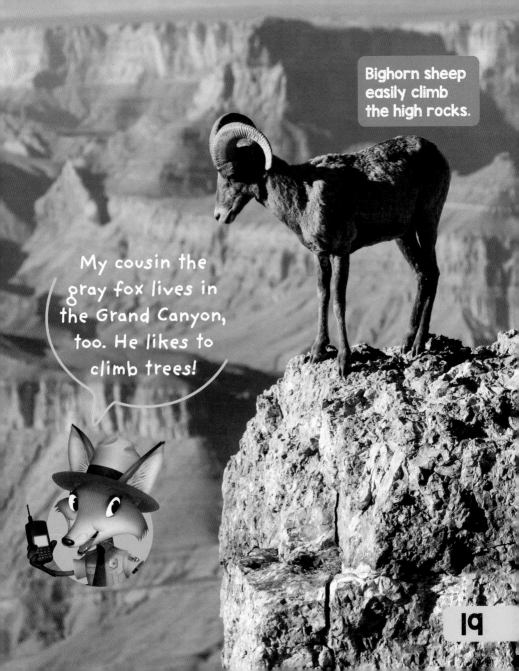

Bighorn sheep easily climb the high rocks.

My cousin the gray fox lives in the Grand Canyon, too. He likes to climb trees!

19

Don't forget to look up! You may see a woodpecker, raven, or hummingbird overhead. Hawks, falcons, and eagles soar above the canyon. If you are lucky, you may even spot a rare California condor.

The California condor has the largest wingspan of any bird in North America. It is almost 10 feet (3 meters).

Hummingbirds feed on the nectar of wildflowers.

Chapter 4

Going to Extremes

If you visit the Grand Canyon, you will have lots of company. It is a popular spot. Many people hike, fish, and camp. Adventure seekers can journey to remote waterfalls. They can also fly overhead in a helicopter, or raft along the Colorado River.

The Colorado River is the sixth-longest river in the U.S.

Rafting on the Colorado River can be a wild ride!

You can even see the canyon from a glass-bottom walkway. The Grand Canyon Skywalk is just outside the park. It juts off the canyon's edge. The Hualapai (**wall**-uh-pie) tribe built the skywalk. It is a grand part of a Grand Canyon adventure!

Imagine you could visit the Grand Canyon. What would you do there?

The Hualapai
are American
Indians that live
in the area.

These are just some of the incredible animals that make their home in the Grand Canyon.

Abert's squirrel

raven

bobcat

porcupine

coyote

California condor

mule deer

Wildlife by the Numbers

The park is home to about...

450 types of birds   **91** types of mammals

More than 22 species of bats live in the Grand Canyon!

elk

cottontail rabbit

bighorn sheep

chuckwalla lizard

rainbow trout

little brown bat

golden eagle

ringtail

rattlesnake

58 types of reptiles and amphibians

24 types of fish

Oh no! Ranger Red Fox has lost his way in the park. But you can help. Use the map and the clues below to find him.

1. Ranger Red Fox took a nap near the Visitor Center on the South Rim.

2. When he woke up, he walked northeast to Mather Point.

3. Then he trotted west to see the view from Hopi Point.

4. Finally, he hiked east. He climbed the stairs up a stone building. Now he is enjoying a spectacular view of the canyon!

Help! Can you find me?

UTAH

Lake Powell

ARIZONA

Desert View
Watchtower

North
Rim

Colorado River

Hopi Point

South
Rim

Visitor
Center

Mather Point

U.S.

Area of map

Alaska and Hawaii are not drawn to
scale or placed in their proper places.

Compass Rose

North

West ◆ East

South

Can you guess which leaf belongs to which tree in the Grand Canyon? Read the clues to help you.

A.

B.

1. Pinyon pine
Clue: This tree has short, curved needles. Stubby cones grow on its branches.

2. Quaking aspen
Clue: Its leaves are almost heart-shaped. They turn gold in fall. The slightest breeze makes them flutter or quake.

3. Big sagebrush
Clue: Its small leaves look grayish green. Their tips are divided into three lobes.

D.

4. Utah juniper
Clue: Short, spiny leaves grow from its branches. Bluish cones called berries hang from them.

C.

Answers: 1. C; 2. A; 3. D; 4. B

Glossary

canyon (**kan**-yuhn): deep, narrow river valley with steep sides

crevices (**krev**-iss-es): narrow openings in rocks

national park (**nash**-uh-nuhl pahrk): area where the land and its animals are protected by the U.S. government

rim (**rim**): border or outside edge of something round or curved

Index

Facts for Now

Visit this Scholastic Web site for more information
on Grand Canyon National Park
www.factsfornow.scholastic.com
Enter the keywords **Grand Canyon**

About the Author

Lisa M. Herrington has written many books for kids. She loved exploring the Grand Canyon. During her trip, she spotted mule deer, cottontail rabbits, eagles, and other interesting animals. Lisa lives in Connecticut with her husband and daughter.